About the Author

Christopher J. Steele is an eminent educator and potter who taught at Desborough School for 33 years before retirement in 2012. He taught Photography, Art and Pottery and now has a studio where he produces hand thrown and sculptural ceramics. This small volume celebrates his art and love for natures beauty.

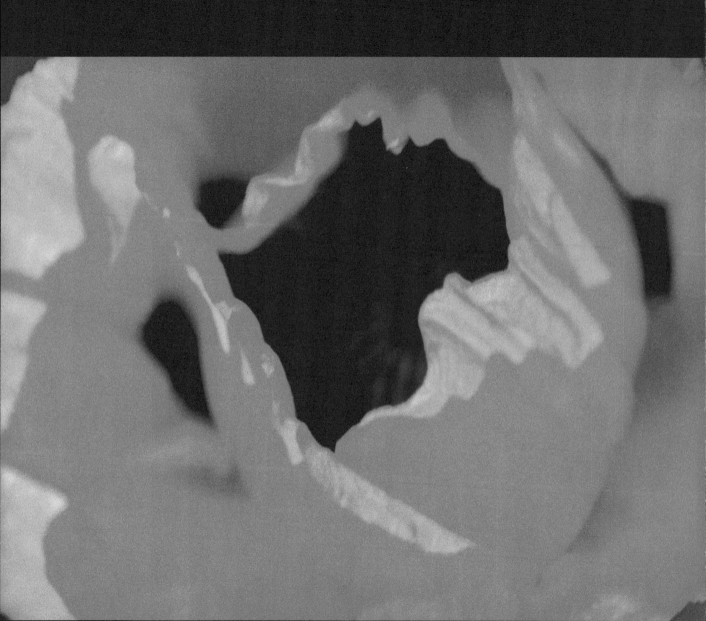

Dedication

The following images and thoughts are dedicated to
my family, who I deeply love and cherish.

A CIP catalogue record for this title is available from the British Library.

First Edition Published: 2016 (Austin Macauley Publishers ™ Ltd)

ISBN 9781528925327 (Paperback)
ISBN 9781528925310 (Hardback)
ISBN 9781528925297 (Kindle Ebook)

www.austinmacauley.com

This Edition Published (2018)
Austin Macauley Publishers ™Ltd.
25 Canada Square
Canary Wharf
London
E14 5LQ

AUSTIN MACAULEY PUBLISHERS™
LONDON • CAMBRIDGE • NEW YORK • SHARJAH

Printed and bound in Great Britain

My love is deeper
than the wells of
your bright eyes.
It shines and twinkles
like a galaxy of stars.
My heart burns with
passion and desire.
One word or glance from
you sends me into a spin;
freefalling to heaven,
taking over my mind.

Nightingales blush
hearing your dulcet
tones, ringing my heart
strings like an angel's
harp. Choirs' angels sell
their souls to reach your
melodies. The charm and
sweetness of your voice
melt my heart and mind.
I now know heaven's
sounds when I hear you.

Your kindess kisses my
heart; its bounds are
unlimited. If you owned
the world you would gift
it away. Generous to a
fault, your heart is an
ocean full of treasures.
My admiration knows no
earthly bounds. My spirits
fly high when you
are nigh.

Your friendship is like a galaxy of stars, bright and deep, shining, glowing, burning bright. Its complexity sparks my heart and soul. Without you I'd be lost in space; a black vacuum would consume me. A void would eat my mind like a black hole in the universe.

Athena, Helen of Troy, and Cleopatra are legends of love and intrigue. Goddesses and Queens have to retreat as you are no myth. To me your spirit is higher than all of them combined. All mortals should cry in joy when your presence is felt.

A sweet child, loving and kind, innocent, fresh and full of grace, matches your fairness. You show the world how to act, your diplomacy, supreme tact and cunning show a foxy wile. A look, a smile, say boundless words, encompassing proactive meanings.

I tremble in fear as your temper rages, cutting through my heart and soul like a scalpel's edge. Scathing words rip my mind to shreds as your mood slashes and cuts to a quick. I retch and seethe as you lambast my actions past. I wish to bury myself deep to avoid your torment's embrace.

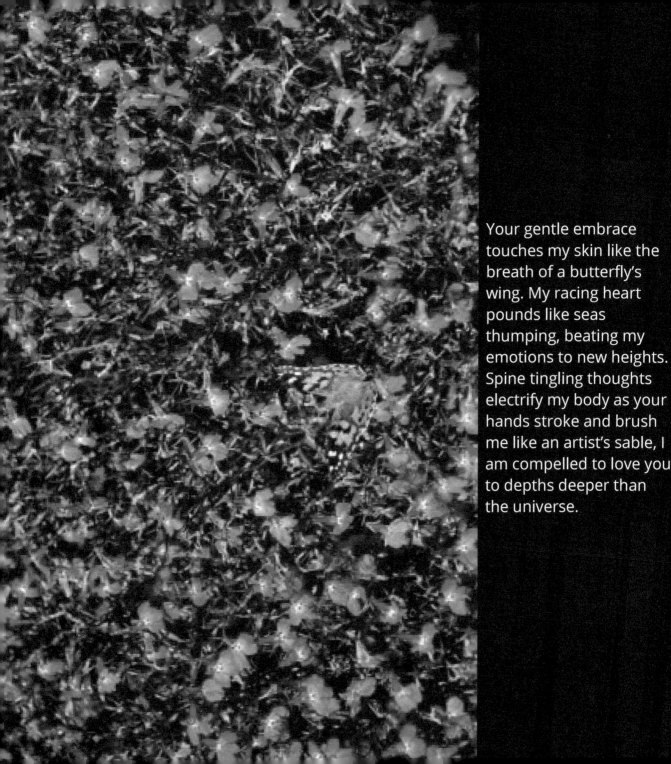

Your gentle embrace touches my skin like the breath of a butterfly's wing. My racing heart pounds like seas thumping, beating my emotions to new heights. Spine tingling thoughts electrify my body as your hands stroke and brush me like an artist's sable, I am compelled to love you to depths deeper than the universe.

To defend you, I'd fight armies of foes. Your worth is beyond all, the richness of your soul goes deeper than diamonds mined, gold and silver shine bright but dull to matt when compared to your preciousness. I value and treasure dear, all the goodness you possess.

Keep the world; all the
brightest diamonds,
jewels and treasures,
I value you more than
wealth unlimited. You
melt hearts of stone with
your presence, intense
as a furnace's heat.

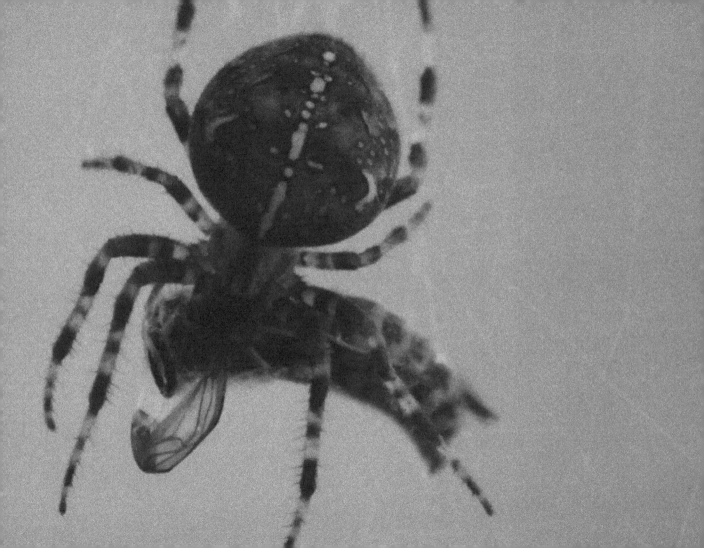

Devils dally with you,
showing no reaction
to your charm. You
mean no harm to their
temptation as they flirt
rapturously. Euphoria and
ecstasy are transmitted
by your ardent desire for
passionate embrace. To
hold you near rings my
heart like an
angelic symphony.

Your heart is warmer than the sun's fierce rays on a bright summer day. It melts my spirit to jelly and ignites my soul, which glows bright in your presence. The fiery power you possess fires my love like a kiln's force, hardening and strengthening its contents.

To be with you, time freezes. Moments are caught, bringing rapturous delights. Memories and images of feelings deep surge like tidal waves breaking, thrusting and rolling my love for you. Experiences past penetrate deep, carving and sculpting channels through my mind, leaving indelible images etched into my consciousness.

Heaven sent you to the world to bring cheer and grace. Your subtle ways change my mind, my heart races boundlessly, championing my ardour. I smile and I sigh; being at one with you is a pure treasure to cherish high.

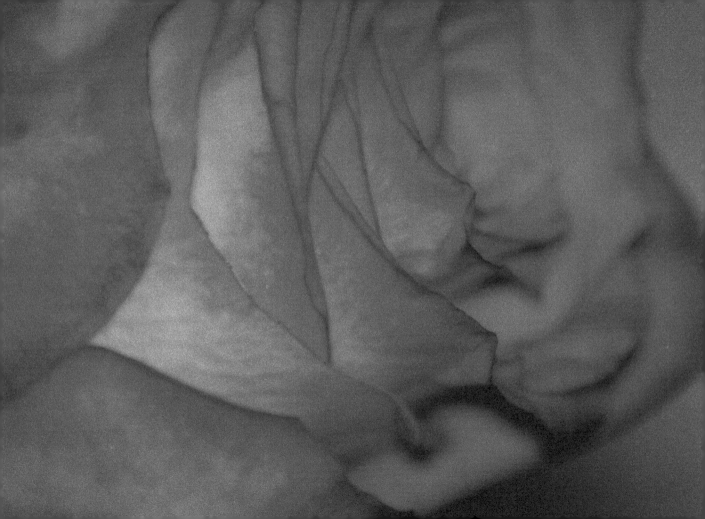

You sharpen my mind to a razor's edge. My imagination deepens to depths unseen. Your presence near me sends all my senses into a quandary; jumping, springing, leaping, pounding with arrows from a thousand angel's bows, all spurned by Eros.

Your soft velvet
complexion rivals finest
silk, petals and halcyon
feathers. I dream of your
sweet embrace, to caress
your body in lovers twine
- be mine for a transient
time! Your skin cushions
my sensuous frame
like a luxurious fantasy
enveloping my soul.

The aroma of your scent spins my mind around faster than a merry-go-round. My pounding heart beats rhythms new, pulses stronger than an army flow. Every nerve is electrified by your closeness. My passionate desire, tempered and washed by your beauty, rivals nature's grace.

CPSIA information can be obtained
at www.ICGtesting.com
Printed in the USA
LVHW081125180423
744493LV00024B/425